2/16/78

MW01033957

ERNEST HOLMES, THE MAN

ERNEST HOLMES
THE MAN

REGINALD C. ARMOR

Science of Mind Publications
Los Angeles, California

First Printing—January 1977

Published by SCIENCE OF MIND PUBLICATIONS
3251 West Sixth Street—P.O. Box 75127
Los Angeles, California 90075
Copyright © 1977 by Reginald C. Armor
All Rights Reserved
Printed in the United States of America
ISBN 0-911336-66-4

To Ernest Holmes, my lifelong friend and co-worker, who inspired this book;

To my wife, Elsie, also a friend of Ernest Holmes, whose persistent, gentle urgings and loving help assisted so much in the work that made this book possible;

To my colleagues who also knew and worked with Ernest, and who offered many helpful suggestions . . .

this book is lovingly dedicated.

ACKNOWLEDGEMENTS

I offer special thanks to my secretary, Robbie Owens, who supervised the mechanical aspects of typing and assembling the material for this book;

And to Willis Kinnear, longtime Editor (now Editor Emeritus) of *Science of Mind* Magazine, friend and confidant of Ernest Holmes for many years, I express my appreciation for his encouragement during my preparation of this manuscript.

Also by Reginald C. Armor

BOOKS

The Magic of Love
Mind Does It
Thought Is Power
Very Present Help

MISCELLANEOUS

Coauthor with Ernest Holmes,
The Forty-eight Lesson
Accredited Study Course in
The Science of Mind

Recorded Lesson Series (cassette)
"Steps to Understanding"

CONTENTS

The author in his Boy Scout uniform, about two years after he met Ernest.

Ernest in 1915, the year his friendship with the author began.

INTRODUCTION

From time to time, there appear among us those people of apparent genius, people whose insight, understanding, and love are influential in changing the thinking of whole generations, and whose impact will be felt for years to come. I sincerely believe Ernest Holmes to have been such a person.

Because I knew Ernest intimately for 45 years (I met him when I was 12 years old and he was 27), I was aware of the deep sincerity of his search for answers to basic questions about life. This search led him to study science, philosophy, and religion, as firsthand he sought out the great minds in these various fields. His investigations took him to authorities on psychology, philosophy, psychosomatic medicine, faith healing, spiritualism, psychic phenomena, and many other related areas.

Throughout all of this investigation, the desire uppermost in his mind was to synthesize what he learned, to "put it all together" into one practical, usable philosophy which also would be the basis of a satisfying way of life. That he succeeded in great measure in this, his great goal, is evidenced, I believe, by the countless thousands throughout the world who follow his teachings, and by the tremendous influence those teachings continue to have on researches in many areas of contemporary thought.

I knew Ernest to be a very balanced person, for while he was seeking constantly to understand the hidden, unseen side of life, he was also an extroverted man who sensed that life was to be lived, enjoyed, and shared with others. "In the living of life," he said, "we are expressing the only purpose there would seem to be for man's existence."

From early childhood, he was convinced of the Beingness of God, expressing as Spirit and as Universal Law— as the Presence and the Power. These were instinctive realizations which prompted him unceasingly to seek verifying answers from every source. What is God? What is life? What is man and his place in the scheme of things? Such questions constantly stimulated his quest for truth.

Ernest realized that neither he nor anyone else would ever have the final answers to these timeless inquiries. "Man will never encompass the Infinite," he said, "for to do so would make him God, which is an impossibility." However, he recognized that true wisdom and enlightenment are not concerned with knowing everything, but with evolving in continuous spiritual unfoldment from plateau to plateau, and he knew that throughout history when others had asked the same questions about Life, they had received insights into some satisfying answers. And as he avidly studied the great religions of the world as well as the great philosophies and the sciences, his researches led him to ideas and conclusions identical to those reached by great souls throughout the ages: that there is an inside, unseen world of causation, from which stems the objective world; and that this inside and the outside are both aspects of the wholeness of God, expressing. Ernest made no claim to having personally discovered any great truth, but through his thoughtful approach to metaphysical studies, he added his own insights to the opinions of the great, the good, and the wise of all ages. In particular, he contributed to the world the technique which he called "spiritual mind treatment."

Being very practical, he always submitted his insights, contemplations, and feelings to his reasoning, intellectual mind for verification. He knew that the evidence of his senses was not to be denied, because it is the world of senses where we live physically. Some insights may call for an explanation or clarification in relation to the time-space universe in which we function, but they will never deny its existence, for this is what religion and man's search for God are all about. "Keep faith with reason," he always said. However, Ernest knew that while his intellectual inquiry was necessary, its purpose was to reach a point in awareness, or consciousness, beyond the intellect, one that would establish a firm faith in God, a God of Good and of Love.

His constant search led him to feel very close to the Infinite Presence. He spent many hours and often days in meditation and communion with It. He believed firmly that everyone can commune with this Presence, talk to It, and receive definite guidance in their lives.

His feelings at such times of meditation and communion, he said, could not be described in words. Those feel-

4

ings convinced him, though, of the oneness of all things, the certainty of the fact that all people are Divine beings, and that every individual is immortal. In his moments of contemplation, insights came to him that opened the door of his mind to intimate contact with the Reality and Truth of Life, and he became sure that there is a Creative Principle operating in and through all creation, a Principle that acts as the Law of Cause and Effect, of Action and Reaction.

He also sensed a warm response on the part of Spirit, one that went far beyond intellectual comprehension, and he experienced this Presence as an understanding Love on the part of the Infinite. He said, "God is not only a hard, cold Principle, but is also a warm, loving Presence which, by nature, desires only good for man." Those insights which resulted from moments of aloneness in contemplation, meditation, and communion with the Presence so convinced him of this all-inclusive wholeness of Life that nothing could shake his conviction.

To the end of his expression on this plane of experience, he constantly searched for new plateaus of understanding and wisdom, always keeping in his mind his lifelong premise, "There is only one Life and one Law, from which all things come."

In his later years, in those many hours each day of meditation, some of his experiences bordered on the purely mystical, and I am sure he was aware of flashes of so-called cosmic consciousness.* These experiences further con-

*One such spontaneous experience occurred during a public meeting as Ernest was giving the dedicatory address at Christ Church of Religious Science in Whittier, California, February 12, 1959. Fortunately, this

firmed his faith, his certainty in regard to the convictions at which he arrived through his intellectual search.

He did not talk about these glimpses of Reality and would not admit to being classified as a mystic, but his inspirational writings are evidence that, in truth, he was. One reason for his reluctance to talk about his mystical sense and the flashes of insight, particularly those that might have actually been cosmic consciousness, was that he wanted to keep his philosophy and the teaching of it at a level which the greatest number of people would understand. He always said, "Keep it simple!" Also, he did not wish to be misunderstood or thought of as anything but a natural, normal human being. "All men are Divine beings, with not too much difference between the highest and the lowest on the scale of development seen from the overall view of Infinity," he would say.

I believe it was this inner awareness which was felt, consciously or subconsciously, by all who contacted him, listened to his lectures, or studied his works. I often thought that his listeners were getting the mental atmosphere of the man, that inner awareness, rather than whatever words he was speaking.

With all of his love for humanity and reverence for God, Ernest Holmes was a very practical man. Coming from New England as he had, he thought of his practicality as "Yankee good-business judgment." He generally knew if and when people lied to him, but he did not condemn them for

_____

unusual event was tape recorded, and though Ernest, himself, never referred to the incident publicly, the transcript was published post-humously in the 1971 Science of Mind Publications book, Light.

it, knowing no one could take advantage of him in a hurtful manner. He was certain that his own understanding and work with spiritual mind treatment would take care of any situation, and that right answers would come from whatever source was appropriate.

He also had the ability to look through appearance to the reality or truth behind it. He viewed the imperfect man and saw the real God-man. "This," he said, "is judging righteously, and not according to appearance."

Ernest was a "practical idealist and an idealistic realist." He was a person who saw God in all things, who could soar to metaphysical heights in speech or meditation and then, at the next moment, enter the experiences of everyday life—laughing, telling a good story, or concocting some new culinary marvel. It was these qualities of humanness and of balance which made him the great man he was. However, Ernest refused to let anyone put him on a pedestal. He said, "All are rooted in the living of life and you will discover all have feet of clay."

While it was primarily his commonsense, down-to-earth manner which attracted people to him personally and caused him to be so greatly loved, the essence of his personal appeal went deeper than that. I am sure that throughout his dealings with others there was always an atmosphere in the situation which was a reflection of his dedication to and love of Truth, for one thing is certain: Ernest Holmes practiced what he preached. He was always seeking to express outwardly his inner feelings and convictions. He laughed and was very happy. He loved greatly, and was greatly loved by all, even those who did not agree with his ideas and opinions. He knew there was good in all things. If he didn't see it immediately, he deliberately pierced the shell of appearance and sensed the God-Presence which is always there.

Those who knew him personally, even if the acquaintance was a casual one, recognized him as a man of great personal charm. He radiated a warmth, sureness, and certainty which left one with a feeling of well-being and uplift, even though few words were spoken. One's inner reaction usually was, "Here is a great man. A man of depth of thought and warm understanding." The atmosphere which he imparted was inspiring and made one feel it is good to be alive, and good to know this wonderful person. He often caused those who met him or talked to him to feel that he was one of their best friends.

To the countless thousands who did not have the privilege of meeting or knowing him personally, but who have read his books and studied his teaching, Ernest is revered as a great teacher and a man of profound insight, one whose ability to grasp basic truths about the nature of God, man, and life was phenomenal. But what of Ernest Holmes, the man? Who was the man behind the teaching? This book, intended to emphasize his human side, illustrates something of the way I knew him to be personally.

Aware of his true humility and refusal to be put on a pedestal, I feel this presentation would have his complete approval. And while I have taken instances and situations which are primarily reflective of his human side, I am sure that his depth of thought and insight will be evidenced in these examples. In addition, using the many years of our close contact as a background, I have sought to elaborate on what I know his feelings to have been about certain of the examples. In some of them, the meaning of the truism, "Many a truth is spoken in jest," is justified.

Because my family's home was located adjacent to Ernest's home, fondly called "The Hill," in Palms, California, our association with Ernest was a loving family relationship. Both Mrs. Armor and I are well aware of and appreciate the influence he had on our growing family of Reggie, Marilyn, and Dorothy during their formative years, one which has meant so much to them in adult life. Ernest's love, thoughtfulness, and wise counsel will live with them forever.

Personally, I am extremely grateful for the privilege of having known him intimately over a period of 45 years, sharing with him his endeavors to make the findings of his search available to an increasing number of persons throughout the world.

I trust that the many students and followers of his teachings will, during the years to come, have an insight into the whole man, feeling they know Ernest Holmes more intimately as a result of this compendium. I am sure that would be his great desire.

ERNEST HOLMES, THE MAN

Section One
ANECDOTES AND SAYINGS

ON THE ABSOLUTE—"The Absolute is a much misinterpreted, much misunderstood term. I think of It as the All-in-All, which was never created and really has no reason for being except that It is. We can't get *into* the Absolute, which some people feel they must do in meditation or spirtual mind treatment, because we are already there. And we cannot describe the Absolute because to do so we must use relative terms."

Ernest felt that there is a place within each one of us where there is a Power which is all-powerful, unconditioned, and which is not affected by outer circumstances or appearances. This, he said, is First Cause, or pure Spirit, which we are constantly using for specific purposes in our life. The real God-man has his roots in this residence Place— the Holy of Holies—and is forever perfect, regardless of outer appearances.

ON RECEIVING THE DIVINE GIFTS—"It is the nature of the Divine, or God, to give of Himself, fully and completely. There is *much to be received,* but there is also *much to be surrendered.*"

In his thinking about the "ever-availability of Good," Ernest often used the statement above. He felt that the Divine gift has been made, but, as with any gift, it must be received. In his saying, "much to be surrendered," I am sure he had in mind Emerson's admonition that we should "take our bloated nothingness out of the path of the divine circuits." This "nothingness" is surely the egocentric opinions we have of ourselves, the limiting ideas or preconceived opinions.

Ernest felt that before the gifts of God could really be received, man would be required to surrender some of his little ideas of limitation to the inspiration of a Divine awareness within; that man should seek to let the Divine reveal to him that which he should know and do, to bring into his experience the greater good which he desires.

ON INFINITY—"Infinity must be what Reality is. You cannot have an Infinite which is snipped off at either end, because God never had a beginning nor can He ever have an ending. God, or Life, must have always existed and will never cease to be. Although the play of Infinite Life upon Itself is the world of conditions and affairs, behind it is that which never changes, the Infinite Possibility."

Ernest said, "We cannot comprehend with our finite minds actually what Infinity means, but we must accept that It is great. It is all-inclusive and we just move with It as we express ourselves in life." So it is that to live is always to express, bringing more of the Infinite Possibility into our experience. This process is something which must go on forever, even though we do not grasp with our finite minds what that means.

14

ON BEING HUMAN—"Everyone has, by nature, a little 'ham' in him—a little show-off—and likes to perform. I like to ham it up myself—what's more, I love appreciation for the effort I put forth. I have always thought that a little 'taffy' before 'shuffling off' is much better than a lot of 'epitaffy' after one goes on to the new experience. I guess

I just love its giddy gurgle,
I love its fluid flow.
I love to wind my tongue up,
I love to hear it go."

Ernest did, indeed, like to "ham it up." He liked the feel of audience appreciation, particularly when he was reciting dramatic poems. He had a wonderful time on the lecture platform, and he completely enjoyed it. And it is true that he did seem to get a big kick out of talking, talking, talking. He was not, in the main, talking in an aimless way, but he did love to be on the platform as a performer as well as a lecturer.

ON SEARCHING—"There is an instinctive Divine urge within everyone to know more, to be more, and to express more, and (I have found that the thing we are searching *for* is the thing we are searching *with.*)"

Ernest taught that the answers we seek are already in our mind, because we are one with God-Mind, the only Mind there is. As we recognize this fact and are receptive to it, we experience added insight and greater spiritual vision.

According to the teaching of the Science of Mind, there is an exact response of the Law of God-Mind to us, and so it follows that whatever is in our individual subjective mind tends to and finally must reproduce itself in the objective world.

A spiritual mind healing, as understood and taught by Ernest Holmes, is based on this realization—that when we change our ideas, conditions are bound to change. In spiritual mind healing we introduce ideas which are more spiritual (more God-like) to replace those that we feel have caused an outer condition which is unhappy, limited, or not to our liking.

> ON FRUSTRATION—"There is no more frustrated person in this world than a frustrated metaphysician, because the metaphysician has had a glimpse of the greater possibility and he has, actually, more to be frustrated about."

Ernest explained that as we have a glimpse of our true relationship with the Infinite and realize the greater possibility within each of us, we may, in our objective thinking, fall into a trap of impatience and frustration. This same realization, however, will reveal that there is something within us forever unfolding, and if we will recognize it, listen to it, bless it, and let it move through us, it will bring peace of mind and ultimately *remove* any sense of impatience or frustration.

ON HUMILITY—"To be humble does not mean that we must become doormats. True humility, in my estimation, is simply a recognition of our own worth, even as we respect and seek to understand the worthiness of others."

In Ernest's opinion, humility was not self-abnegation. When asked what he would do if someone seemed to excel him in speaking or lecturing, I remember his remarking that, "I would just work mighty hard to improve my own presentation." But, facetiously, he often said, "I recognize no superiors and darned few equals."

ON SELF-ESTEEM—"You are the most wonderful person you will ever know. As a matter of fact, you are the only person you will ever really know, although because you are a God-intended person, your self-awareness permits you to be aware of others and what goes on around you. You are constantly being and expressing that which you know yourself to be."

Ernest explained that this realization is based on a thoughtful recognition of the real Self which is within each of us. Our awareness of this wonderful fact permits us also to know that it is true about every person who lives, and this is the true basis of our being able to love others as ourselves.

17

ON DRINKING HARD LIQUOR —
"There are other ways of getting 'lit up'
besides drinking liquor. Why should I
addle what little brains I have with the
stuff?"

Ernest did not object to others indulging if they felt it necessary. That was their choice. He took a little wine now and
then, but said, "It usually upsets my stomach so why bother
with it."

ON HEAVEN AND HELL—"In my
estimation there are no such places as
the literally accepted ideas of heaven or
hell. It would seem unthinkable and
certainly illogical to believe that such
states could be created by God. I think
that what we call 'hell' is a condition
of experience on this plane which 'exists only but for the lack of an idea of
heaven.' I do not believe that anyone
can be forever damned or committed to
a place which has been called the literal
hell. Nor do I believe that one can be
consigned to the boredom of a state of
eternal bliss called heaven."

Ernest thought that either through our power of choice or
an unconscious acceptance, we create those experiences
which we define as "hell." They are the result of our natural human mistakes and are not to be considered the result of Divine will or purpose. He said he wasn't bothered

18

by the appearance of these experiences—the low depressive states which we might call "hell"—because he believed it is the destiny of man to discover for himself the truth about himself, his Divine Sonship, his Oneness with God and Life, and those experiences were the ways we chose to make that discovery. He said that in spite of its problems and the so-called "hellish" things humanity seems to be going through, mankind is "hell-bent for heaven."

ON BIBLE INTERPRETATION—"I have found that Bible interpretation is often the reflection of a personal opinion—more a matter of reading something *into* the Bible rather than getting something *out* of it. Acceptance of the legitimate symbology in the sacred writings has become a powerful influence on human thought which has been accepted throughout the ages, but in reading the Bible one should draw his own conclusions and interpret them in the light of his own understanding. In this way, it becomes personal to him."

Ernest knew that at various times in history there were persons whose sincere interpretations of the Bible have been accepted by many people. These interpretations were believed in, were accepted, and in this manner became very powerfully incorporated in the race belief. But he also knew that much of the truth in the Bible was written in story form or as allegory, simply to hide it from those in political authority who, at the time, might have taken exception to its revelation. This is why it is necessary that each person interpret the Bible according to his own understanding of the symbols and stories, rather than to take everything literally.

ON THEOLOGY—"I believe that theology in its generally accepted form is simply a collection of opinions propounded by certain religionists; opinions which have been accepted, believed in, and also have changed from time to time. Often they have been proclaimed as revelations of God.

"I have opinions, too. They come from the same Source as those of the greatest theologians, and that is the One Source."

Ernest sought out the premier theologians of his time, but I have known him to tell them, "I have a brand of theology which, in my estimation, is just as valid as yours." Often he would paraphrase Emerson, remarking that "Theology, in my view, comprises the mumps, measles, and chicken pox of religion."

ON COOKING—"I just love to cook. I never cook by recipe. Being creative, I guess I just like to use my imagination and put things together. As any creative chef would do, I constantly sample as I go. In my early days, I was a 'bootcher' [this is what it sounded like in his New England accent] you know, and I still just love to see what I can do with meat. I love meat—I like to see how I can flavor it, how I can cook it. And I'm always anxious to see just how the whole thing's going to turn out."

Ernest often had a number of guests for dinner. He would invite eight or ten people after a Sunday lecture, saying, "Come on home with me and have dinner. I've got a big pot of stew just waiting."

His belief in the universality of substance and supply showed up in his preparation of food. He was always very generous in his cooking and usually prepared twice as much food as he would need. Most of his dishes were a sort of stew, and he prepared all kinds. For one of his favorites, a fish chowder, he would get fresh fish, put in some bacon, potatoes, onions, milk, and pork fat, and let it simmer. Being from New England, he naturally loved to cook this chowder, and it really was delicious.

In connection with his cooking, he got a great kick out of talking to different people, comparing how they prepared various foods. Firsthand, I know Ernest was a very good cook, as he often supplied Mrs. Armor and me with surplus quantities of the tasty dishes he had prepared.

ON MENTAL INFLUENCE—"No one has the right to influence another person as to what to do or to think. God created man a Divine Being with the power of discernment and choice, and this ability means he can consciously make decisions and create his own destiny; even God doesn't tell man how he shall think. As a Divine individual, man is let alone to discover the truth about himself, and so in Religious Science, in our healing work, we never seek to influence another person—mentally or any other way. To do this would be a violation of his God-given prerogative of self-choice."

Ernest felt this realization completely in his spiritual mind practice. He said, "It is never a matter of mental influence. In formulating our treatments, we are simply knowing the Truth about people, but not wondering how It is going to reach them, or when It will. This is a basic tenet in our metaphysical technique. Even in using the words of treatment, we never speak directly to our patient—we never say 'you are.' We simply know something about the self. We can say, 'I am,' or 'God-man is,' or 'so-and-so is.' This is the proper technique, for it includes a perfect recognition of the other's Divine individuality."

ON MATERIAL GIFTS—"The gift is always greatest to the giver. Give the best that you have, always, and the best

will come back to you. This is the Law
of God-Mind in action."

Ernest used a similar type of statement when he said,
"Money has no home." He believed that when money is
circulated its good is multiplied manyfold. We should keep
our good flowing to us by gratefully receiving the gifts of
money or any material things, using them, and, in turn,
passing them along for others to enjoy.

He evidenced this in his life. He would often buy a shirt, a
tie, or a jacket, and wear it just a few times and then pass
it along to a friend, saying, "I think this would look very
good on you." He loved to do this in all ways and with all
things, including money. He did not give foolishly, and he
did not give simply to enhance his ego. He gave in a spirit
which understands the necessity of circulating Divine Substance. He knew and proved continually that whatever he
gave came back to him in "good measure, pressed down,
and shaken together, and running over . . . ."

ON CRITICISM—"I never criticize—I
only analyze. What others do is their
business and I may disagree but it is
still their problem. If I criticize or pass
judgment on their actions, on what
they do, then it becomes my problem
and does not help the situation in any
way."

Ernest frequently said, "I never criticize—I only analyze."
And he would also say the same words with tongue-in-

cheek, adding, "If that isn't a classic example of rationalizing, I never saw one." He tried to follow his belief of not criticizing, but admitted that it was difficult for him at times when he was personally involved.

Being positive-minded, he was inclined to think in terms of how he would act or respond in another's situation. Knowing the nature of Law, he sought to be kind in his suggestions or criticisms, respecting another's right to act in freedom—and he expected this understanding treatment from others. He did not accept negative criticism from any source, and sought always to avoid offering this type of criticism, even though it might have been excusable under the guise of "constructive criticism."

ON TEACHING THE SCIENCE OF
MIND—"You always have to place the
fodder where the horse can reach it."

When he made this statement, he would often jokingly add that he was not saying that his audience was a bunch of jackasses. It was just his simple way of stating that he believed the teaching should be presented as simply as possible and in language understandable to those to whom it was being taught. One of his favorite statements was, "Let's keep it simple."

ON FACTS AND EXPERIENCES—
"We should never deny the evidence of
our senses or the facts as they appear.

24

They are always as real as they are sup-
posed to be. We should know, however,
they are never entities of themselves.
That which brings them into being,
their cause, can always be changed, es-
tablishing a new set of apparent facts.
Facts are not nonexistent illusions of
our mind. The illusion is never in the
objective fact or experience but is always in our interpretation of the fact or
experience. Are they real, permanent,
and unchangeable, or can they be
changed? The answer to this question
will reveal an important fact regarding
facts."

Wisdom, or spiritual insights within us, enables us to see
through facts and experiences to the Truth about them. Insight will then enable us to set up a *new* set of facts or
experiences, because we are always setting in motion the
creative Power which established and sustained the first fact
or experience.

ON PHYSICAL EXERCISE—"I'm not
much of an exercise enthusiast but my
favorite exercise is—" and he would
raise his two index fingers and bend
them at the knuckles back and forth
several times.

As a matter of fact, Ernest did like to exercise and his favorite was walking with a cane, preferably in a busy, big
city street. He said, "That's where the action is, and I like
action." He also liked gardening in a limited way, with

potted plants and flower beds his favorites. In his gardening, he was very kind to the plants and often admitted, "I just feed them to death," which of course sometimes happened. He loved to use the fertilizer because he thought they liked it and oftentimes would be too generous in his use of it, which didn't work out too well with the plants.

> ON WISDOM—"In our contacts with life and people, and in our use of the Law of Mind, we should be 'wise as serpents, and harmless as doves.' "

Ernest felt that there is no substitute for wisdom and love in our attitudes. He stated that in talking with someone, he would often know intuitively when the person was lying. To him such a recognition was the *wisdom of the serpent,* but the fact that he understood, did not quarrel with, or even tell the person he knew he was being lied to, was being as *harmless as a dove.*

During his lifetime this was a rule of thumb which he sought always to follow in his contacts with people and his constructive use of the Law of God-Mind.

> ON HYPNOTISM—"I believe the phenomenon of hypnotism is real. It demonstrates the universality of the medium of subjective Mind, the Oneness of Mind, and man's existence within that Mind. But I believe that hypnotism as it is sometimes practiced is a psychological crime against the individual. I

26

say this because it often involves sur-
rendering one's conscious mental faculties, knowingly, to another person. It
becomes, in essence, the usurping of
these faculties by another, turning them
over willingly, or, in some instances,
unwillingly. In any event, at that level
it is a state of mental coercion or mental domination, lessening or eliminat-
ing one's power of choice. In the hands
of a trained therapist, hypnotism may,
in some instances, be beneficial, but it
is not a phenomenon to be experi-
mented with by those who are novices
or who do not understand all the impli-
cations involved."

Ernest was very specific in stating that man's self-awareness
represents his Divine individuality and that no one has the
right to usurp this. In the case of hypnotism, we do, to
some degree, surrender this individuality to another person,
either consciously or unconsciously, and Ernest believed
this is not a good habit to get into. Our power of choice
is something to be guarded closely and zealously since it
is God-given, and "even God, Himself, does not attempt
to coerce the individual."

ON AGING—"The body is made of
Divine Substance, the eternal Substance of God, and as such, it is constantly renewing itself after the spiritual
pattern, or prototype, in the Mind of

27

God. Both the Spirit and God-Sub-
stance as we understand it are individualized as ourselves. In Truth, then,
we are eternal beings. We should live
as long as we wish on this plane, and
certainly while we live, we should enjoy
life. When we come to that place in living where there is less to look forward to
than there has been in the past, then it
would seem that something in us begins
to change. This is the aging process. In
the human, with the power of choice, it
is largely a matter of his own volition."

Ernest had no patience with the idea of living on if he
couldn't enjoy being alive and experiencing the joy and
happiness which he always believed in so thoroughly. I recall one evening when he and Hazel were walking down the
sidewalk and saw before them a bent little old man, and
he said to her. "If I ever get in that shape, I want you
to slip something in my coffee that will help me move
quickly on to the new experience of living." He was so full
of life himself and so full of enthusiasm about living that
he didn't see any sense in living on this plane of experience beyond the time when one had ceased to be genuinely
enthused about it.

ON ATTENDING A SPIRITUAL RE-
TREAT—"I have no quarrel with the
idea of spiritual retreat for those people
who want one and feel they need it. For
myself, I want to be in the middle of

28

the activities of life. On my visitations, lectures, and travels, the busiest hotel and busiest part of town suit me fine. Life is to be lived, all of it, in my estimation. I have a spiritual retreat within me, to which I can instantly turn in any circumstance."

He did not like the term "retreat" in its generally accepted meaning. He said, "If they would only call it 'advance' instead of 'retreat' I would be more interested." He did like to take rest periods in his office or home, and he recognized the value of renewal in this process.

He enjoyed communing with nature on vacation trips and he drank deeply of the quietness he might find in a cathedral. I saw him sit for a long period of time in St. Patrick's Cathedral, in New York, meditating in its atmosphere. He also enjoyed the murmur of a mountain stream as he sat on its bank. But it was the required, often regimented routine of the conventional retreat that he would have no part of. He felt we could have our moments of relaxation, contemplation, and meditation by ourselves at any time, in any suitable location.

ON BEING A MECHANIC—"I know nothing whatever about mechanical things. Not having a mechanical turn of mind, I don't know the difference between a spark plug and a carburetor. But then I guess a mechanic wouldn't feel comfortable giving an inspirational talk on Sunday morning."

Ernest never thought of man as an individual separated from the wholeness of God, or Spirit. Believing man to be an individualized expression of God, he knew that each person embodies some special aspect of God as a unique talent, all his own. In this way, every person becomes a dispenser of the Divine gifts of God to others, for their blessing and good. So he did not feel frustrated or inferior because he didn't understand mechanics as well as he did many other things. If the need arose, he would call upon experts for help, those who were trained in their fields, to take care of the particular need. He felt that he didn't have to know all there was to know about everything.

ON THE SUNDAY LECTURE PLAT-FORM—"The *message* of a Sunday talk is the important thing. I want nothing to detract from that—not even beautiful flowers in front of the lectern."

Ernest believed thoroughly in his oneness, at the subjective level, with his audience and with the flow of Spirit as Divine inspiration. He wanted nothing to detract from this flow of communication between his audience, himself, and the ideas of Infinite Spirit. He was not being egotistical, in my estimation. He simply wanted no interference with that rapport which is established between a speaker and an audience, and he felt this rapport strongly in all of his lectures.

Ernest believed that the Sunday services which he conducted for many years were basically teaching lectures, although he did introduce some ideas, such as a hymn for the congregation, or a piano or violin solo that would satisfy those who came for a devotional type of Sunday service. But I remember that on one occasion he said, "You have come here for teaching and inspiration, not to be entertained. If entertainment is what you want, for a reasonable price you can be entertained at a theater."

ON THE SPIRITUAL AND THE MATERIAL — "We live in a spiritual world, peopled by spiritual ideas. There is only One. The seeming difference between the spiritual and material is simply that they are the inside and outside of that one basic Reality, which we call Creation."

Ernest believed that all objective, or material, things are simply God-ideas expressing. They are Spirit in form. He said, "We really cannot tell where one begins and the other leaves off because they are really, in essence, one and the same."

He felt that each of these aspects of the expression of Mind is evidence that the other exists. Without the material, we would have no guarantee that the spiritual world, the ideas of causation, exists. Without the spiritual, the causative ideas, we would have no logical explanation of the material world of effects.

31

ON INCURABLE DISEASES—"There
are, in my opinion, no incurable diseases, but sometimes there are incurable people."

Believing thoroughly in what he taught and in spiritual
mind treatment, Ernest felt that all diseases were curable
through such treatment. He did recognize, however, that
often the complete cures were not realized. When asked to
comment on why this was so, he would sometimes make
the statement quoted above, explaining that quite often
people wanted to be cured "in their sins" rather than "of
their sins." One of his basic beliefs was that while the symp-
toms of disease could be alleviated, a complete healing required a definite change of subjective thought-patterns
through affirmative and constructive thinking. And he
emphasized this principle as the basis for spiritual mind
healing: if you change the cause, then the effect, or healing,
is automatic, as a logical result of the activity of the Law
of God-Mind.

ON GETTING ON CLOUD NINE—
"Do you understand what I am talking
about?" When speaking inspirationally
to a class or Sunday audience, Ernest
occasionally would stop suddenly and
ask this question. When the group
would nod their heads in complete
agreement, he would then say with a
grin, "Well, that's good. I wish to heav-
en I did."

Ernest understood that man is always one with and has access to all of the Presence, Spirit, and Wisdom of God. In his speaking he was aware often that his mind would open to the creative influx of this Divine Presence, and at such times he was aware of Spirit speaking through him at levels far beyond his intellectual understanding at the moment. He believed in this inspirational type of speaking, understanding that he was getting a response according to the preparatory seeds of thought he had previously planted. He said, "Never listen to what you are saying, but say what you are listening to."

> ON HAPPINESS—"I do not believe in a suffering God. The very nature of the Divine is harmony, balance, beauty, and love, evidenced throughout all life and the Universe—and these are qualities that comprise happiness. No man has ever experienced half enough happiness in his life. I am sure that God wants us to be happy. Somehow if we are happy, God is happy about us."

Ernest, by his very nature, was a happy individual, always looking on the affirmative or joyful side of life. His happiness and enthusiasm about people and about life were felt by all who contacted him and resulted in many rewarding contacts and friendships throughout his life.

ON DIRECT PERSONAL REVELA-
TION FROM GOD—"God never whis-
pered anything in my ear that isn't
available for others to hear, also, if they
prepare themselves properly with
prayer and meditation."

Ernest believed in "revelation" in the sense that Infinite
Spirit moves through man upon man's bidding and acceptance, bringing to his conscious attention certain facts and
truths of life. Ernest repeatedly said that God never told
him anything that He wouldn't tell anyone who would take
time to listen, contending that revelation was a matter of
one's desire to receive enlightenment or inspiration on
some given idea. When man places himself in a position to
listen or accept, he opens his mind to receive from Spirit,
that One Source, the desired inspiration or wisdom. Ernest
was always careful to eliminate the idea of superstition from
this process. "Every man," he said, "is a Son of the Most
High and is open to the Infinite at all times."

ON SPIRITUALISM — "I believe we
have to give the spiritualist movement
credit for trying to demonstrate objectively what we, as Religious Scientists,
believe in—that is, the immortality of
the soul and the continuity of life. But I
do not believe that the phenomena experienced in a mediumistic session are
always what they seem to be. In so-
called communication with departed
persons, there is, in my estimation,

definitely a mingling of consciousness of the individual who has gone on and those who are left behind—I believe this is possible and that it often takes place, since there is One Mind and we are all present in that Mind. But in a seance I am not sure that the departed person is always actually *there*. I do believe that a medium has the ability to read, or to interpret, information in the subjective and to make contact at the subjective level with the person who is sitting for a reading, and also with the subjective awareness of the person who has gone on. But I don't believe a medium's ability has anything to do with being spiritual. I think that it is, in a sense, mental gymnastics which anyone could practice and perfect, although some people seem to have a greater ability than others."

Ernest was very interested in spiritualistic mediums and psychic phenomena, but he felt that there was nothing really *spiritual* about these things. The phenomenon itself is very real because of the oneness existing in Mind, but Ernest was never quite satisfied that actual contact was made, even though he did believe that anyone could feel the presence of the one who has gone on if he placed his mind in a certain receptive attitude. After the passing of his beloved wife, Hazel, he tried to establish a definite, conscious contact with her through a medium, but he told me privately after several of these attempts that he was never satisfied. Although "contact" had been achieved, he was never quite convinced that it actually was Hazel who was speaking to him.

ON LETTING GOD SAY "YES" IN TREATMENT — "In spiritual mind treatment, most people have already made up their minds as to how they want God to respond to the treatment."

In speaking of spiritual mind treatment, Ernest said that if one makes up his mind *how* God should answer his prayer, it would be outlining, or telling God what to do. This would open the way for personal opinion to interfere with God Action or Right Action, and in many instances this would be the equivalent of our saying "no" to God's "yes" in a demonstration.

Ernest emphasized the fact that our minds must be open to Divine guidance and to all necessary ideas, or else why treat or pray in the first place? We should know that the right answers to the fulfillment of our needs are known in Infinite Mind, and that Spirit responds to our desire when we eliminate our "no" ideas and say "yes" to God ideas. The attitude that "with God all things are possible" is necessary in letting God say "yes," then what we must do is to get the self, with its preconceived opinions, out of the way long enough to listen to this "yes" from God, to let it move through us.

ON WHAT RELIGIOUS SCIENCE
HAS DONE WITH GOD—"Because I
describe God as infinite, universal, and
exact Law in operation, and describe
what It does, does not mean that I have
left a warm and personal God out of
the picture. God is all there is, of
course, which includes the Law *and* the
Presence."

At times, following one of Ernest's very scientific talks on
the Law of God-Mind and Its exactness of response, someone might comment, "Dr. Holmes, that was a wonderful
intellectual talk you gave and I enjoyed it very much, but I
am wondering, what in the world have you done with God?
Where does He fit into your picture?" I well remember
how Ernest answered: "Thank you very much, and bless
your heart. But we have done nothing in Religious Science
with God, because God is all that we believe in. We believe
in nothing but God. He fits into all pictures, because He is
all pictures. However, we do need to appreciate the beautiful exactness of His Law if we are to believe in His Presence,
His consistency and unfailing response to us individually."

ON INFLATED EGO—"If your inflated ego is showing, and you think you
are something special, stick your finger
in a pail of water, pull it out, and see
how big a hole it leaves."

Even while emphasizing the difference between egotism and
egoism, Ernest understood that we must think well of ourselves. He felt that what we are and feel ourselves to be is

constantly speaking for us in the eyes, ears, and minds of others. He emphasized there will be no danger of becoming *egotistical* if we recognize the high qualities of our own Divine Sonship, also recognizing in others those same qualities.

ON PROPHETS — "There are no prophets but the wise, and every man is a Son of the Most High."

In all of his teaching Ernest sought to be as free as possible from a superstitious approach to Truth. At every opportunity he emphasized the idea that God did not pick out any individual and reveal something exclusively to him.

His statement regarding prophets was, I am sure, prompted by his belief that all men are Divine Beings, with access to the Infinite Spirit of All-Wisdom. He felt the prophets of old were very wise men constantly seeking to live close to God, and that this closeness set up a relationship with the Infinite Spirit, one which manifested as spirtual enlightenment or inspiration within the minds of those prophets. As such a person observed past and present events, this spiritual vision enabled him to sense that certain occurrences would take place in the future as a result of past and present causes that had been set in motion. Ernest felt that this was largely an unconscious knowing, rather than the result of an intellectual process. To him, this made more sense than the idea that God picked out certain individuals to whom He revealed something not available to others, to be expressed as prophecy. It was this understanding that prompted Ernest to say so many times, "God reveals Himself to every man who will listen and who will receive the inspiration of the Almighty."

> ON CHILDREN—"I love all children and feel a deep kinship with the very young. I must confess, however, that I understand those of the age of two or three years a little better than the very small ones. I prefer to let the mothers of the very small children handle them."

Ernest loved all children. While he did seem partial to those who had reached the age when they could consciously and objectively respond to him, he felt a kinship with and loved the little babies as well. He sensed that they were very close to God, having recently left the great Soul-side of life to awaken to self-awareness, and he recognized in infants their responses of love and unquestioned faith in life and God.

I well remember the many christenings he conducted of the very small "babes in arms." He would cuddle them and coo to them and tell them they were Divine Beings expressing God's Love on this plane of experience. And after the christening was over, he would kiss the babies before handing them back to the proud parents.

> ON DUALITY OF BASIC POWERS—"It is illogical and unthinkable that there could be two basic causative

> powers behind creation. If this were
> possible, one would cancel the other
> out and we would have universal chaos
> instead of universal cosmos, which we
> now recognize as a fact."

Ernest insisted that the whole structure of the Science of Mind, or Religious Science, was based on the fact that there is only one basic Power or Reality behind, in, and through all creation. Modern scientific research now recognizes this also. Ernest often mentioned the statement of Einstein that there is one great law governing all things under which all lesser laws come. He also added that "there is one Presence or Spirit in the Universe and all things we see in the objective world are but expressions of that Spirit, the Universal Potential of all ideas."

He emphasized that the co-existence of the One Presence and the One Law does not represent basic duality, but that they are simply aspects of the one absolute or basic Power in action. A misunderstanding of this basic Unity of all things has created seeming duality in the mind of man, which leads to the illusion of heaven and hell, good and bad, and all of the other appearances of "the pairs of opposites." The apparent duality, however, can only be the One, acting within the One, to produce the many manifestations of Itself.

> ON HAVING WHAT YOU WANT—
> "You can have what you want but you
> must be willing to take what goes with
> it."

The Law of God-Mind, according to Its Nature, must give us that which we really want. Ernest emphasized the exactness in response of the Law of Mind to our desire, cautioning that we should, for this reason, use discernment and wisdom in speaking our word for a desired experience. We should be sure it is really what we want!

He suggested the following guidelines: Would its fulfillment benefit all concerned and *be good for us*? Are we willing to accept the necessary details involved in the demonstration of our desire? Will we let go of hatred and jealousy? Will we abandon our refusal to let love of life, of people, and even of ourselves express through us? If we are willing to do these things in any given instance, we are willing to accept our demonstration. Putting it another way, Ernest said, "If we keep our desires on a high level, embodying the essences of good, love, truth, harmony, and so forth, there will be no problem of accepting the responsibility for what goes with God's fulfillment of our word."

ON REINCARNATION—"I have never believed in the commonly accepted idea of reincarnation. The necessity of being reborn into this world, often many times, and going through the growing up process again does not make sense to me. What I do believe in is a straight progression, or unfoldment, of the individual soul—of man's retaining his conscious consciousness when he goes on to enter a new experience of living and self-expression. If I am wrong,

41

what I believe won't make any difference as far as the Truth is concerned.
However, I hope I am right, because I
would not have any desire to go through
the 'diaper' stage again. It would also
seem rather embarrassing to me to be
walking down the street, seeing a little
baby in a baby carriage, and saying to
that youngster, 'Hello, Grandma!' I do
not believe that we must come back
and go through the experience in this
phase of life to make up for the mistakes we have made."

Ernest felt there were other ways of explaining the aspects
of living that seemed to give validity to the idea of reincarnation. Perhaps this experience in the journey of the individualized soul is the first for each of us as a self-conscious
being. Existing in Mind, once we gain this self-awareness,
we move forward from experience to experience, develop-
ing that which we call our individualized identity in the
Universal Spirit, in the Mind of God. Ernest believed that
as Divine Beings we take our complete identity with us to
the next incarnation, for he did believe in *incarnation*. He
believed that we move from one plane of experience in living
to another, maintaining our individuality, but never with
the necessity of having to be reborn as a human.

ON MAN'S PERSONALITY AND HIS
OUTER WORLD OF CONDITIONS
AND AFFAIRS—"If you could take a
picture of a person's subjective mental-

ity, you would find there an exact repro-
duction of his outer world of conditions
and affairs, including his personality."

Ernest emphasized the fact that due to man's ability to
choose, he is constantly creating through the Law of Mind,
not only those conditions and circumstances in which he
lives and functions, but also his actual personality. This
must be true, considering the exactness of response of God-
Mind to one's beliefs.

Ernest said, "If we do not like our outer circumstances,
conditions, or our personality, the place to begin to change
is right within our own mind." He contended this was the
basis of spiritual mind healing and was the process to be
used in bringing about all desired changes in our experience, or in our personality. Change the inner subjective
thought-patterns and acceptances, and the outer world will
automatically change to correspond to these new ideas.

ON BEING YOU—"I believe there is
no individual anything, really. There
are only individualized expressions of
the One, or That which is. Each of us
is individualized and has something
unique to express and to give to Life,
something that is not exactly like the
contribution of anyone else. If two
things in nature *were* exactly alike, or if
two people were alike, one of them
would be superfluous."

Ernest often cited the idea of Emerson that "imitation is suicide," and that we should never try to be like anyone else. He also agreed with Emerson that each individual "should learn to detect and watch that gleam of light which flashes across his mind from within." In other words, he emphasized: Be yourself, for your self is one with the great potential of all ideas of God. You have access to all of those ideas in the expression of your individualized, Divine Self.

In speaking of man, Ernest also emphasized that each person is expressing, in some manner, that which is peculiar to him, and he does a better job at that particular thing than any other individual. No two people are alike—there are no two expressions of God exactly the same in the entire Universe, the potential of God-ideas is limitless, and we individually are important to God, fulfilling a need which is necessary to the wholeness of the Universe.

ON BACKBONE OR WISHBONE —
"In spiritual mind treatment one needs
backbone instead of wishbone."

Ernest referred to the fact that people often form a picture of what they want, but do so by wishful thinking, *hoping* it will come to pass. He knew that such mental activity, which is no more than daydreaming, may produce a good feeling, though it does not necessarily accomplish anything. Certainly it is not the type of thinking which will consistently produce results. He used the terms "wishbone" and "backbone" to illustrate, vividly but without complexity, that there is a great difference between idle hoping, which doesn't get anything done, and having the confidence to speak the word with authority, be persistent, and have affirmative expectancy, and then to follow through by accepting Divine guidance.

ON RELIGION—"I have studied virtually every religion, and I find good in all of them. They are seeking to understand the Power behind all things, which is an instinctive yearning in all people. Furthermore, I believe that any religion one believes in is right for that person at the time he believes in it and seeks to practice its teaching. Ideas do change with the evolving of the human consciousness, and we should recognize that our concepts of religion may also change."

ERNEST HOLMES, THE MAN

Section Two
THE STORYTELLER

Some of His Favorite Jokes and Stories

Because Ernest Holmes was a very natural person, he enjoyed soaring emotionally to great heights in his public lectures and classes. He liked telling a good story as well as listening to one.

In reciting his stories, he always used the gestures and dramatics for which he was well known, acting out the part of whatever characters were involved. In his lectures, when he felt he was becoming too elevated in his thinking, perhaps over the heads of those to whom he was speaking, he deliberately introduced a very mundane story, often to bring them back down to earth. And, of course, these stories frequently had a subtle metaphysical meaning.

So let us now consider some of his favorite tales, remembering particularly that he used whatever theatrics he felt were appropriate for bringing the characters to life.

THE PARTING OF THE WATERS OF THE RED SEA

Visiting his friend's house, a man observed a beautiful picture frame on the wall. But there was no picture in it—just the bare frame. He asked his friend, "What is the meaning of this framed blank canvas?"

"Oh, that is a very special picture of the Egyptians chasing the Israelites across the Red Sea."

Scratching his head, the questioner responded, "But I just don't understand, actually, where the Red Sea *is* in the picture."

"The waters have already parted to allow the Israelites to cross," said the friend.

"Is that so? Well, then, just where are the Israelites?"

"They have already passed over to the other side of the sea."

"Oh, I understand. Well, where are the Egyptians who are chasing the Israelites?"

"Ah ha!" the friend replied, "they haven't yet arrived!"

MAKING BIG TALK

It was a common occurrence that on Monday morning after the Sunday lectures, Ernest would gather with several of the other ministers in the hallway of the Institute of Religious Science and ask them with an impish grin, "Did you make *big talk* yesterday?"

Occasionally one of the ministers replied, "I thought my talk was pretty good. But did *you* make big talk yesterday?"

Ernest would assume one of his quizzical looks and say, "As a matter of fact, I did make *big talk* yesterday. It was so good, I could hardly wait to hear what I was going to say next."

A COLD REMEDY

One of Ernest's favorite stories was that of a boy and girl in New England, where sleigh riding is popular during the cold winters. While riding one Sunday afternoon, bundled up in their blankets, the girl snuggled up to the boy and said, "Johnny, I'm cold."

Johnny looked over to her and said, "I'm cold, too, Jane. Why not tuck in the blankets."

So Jane pulled the blankets closer, but pretty soon she moved even closer to Johnny and said, "My hands are still cold."

He didn't pay much attention to her and soon she nudged him with her elbow and said, "Johnny, did you hear me? My hands are cold . . . and besides nobody loves me."

This time he looked over to her and said, "Jane, remember that God loves you, and you can always sit on your hands to keep them warm."

WHAT TO DO WITH TEXTBOOKS

One of Ernest's pet sayings after the completion of a lesson series with a group of students was this: "You have learned everything that we have to teach you. We have taught you all that we know. Now my advice to you is to throw all your books out the window and actually go out and begin to put into practice what you have learned."

THE CAR THAT WOULDN'T START

A friend of mine told me of an incident that occurred shortly after Ernest had bought a new car. Ernest came to see my friend and after his visit, went out to the new car and pressed the starter. It kept cranking and cranking and cranking, but nothing happened. The motor would not start. After this went on for quite some time the friend, who was standing there watching, chuckling to himself, walked over to the car.

"Ernest, are you having a little difficulty?"

"I just can't get this darn car to start. It's new and I don't understand how it works."

My friend reached over and turned on the ignition switch, after which the car started immediately.

Ernest, who had no understanding of mechanical things, considered this quite a joke on himself and they both had a good laugh about it.

MISTAKEN IDENTITY

There was a psychiatrist who had a patient come in for consultation and treatment. The patient was sitting in a chair in his office, affectionately holding a duck, when the doctor entered and asked, "Good afternoon. Just what is your problem?"

"There really isn't any problem with me, Doctor," she said, stroking the duck. "The problem I came to see you about is with my husband here. He thinks he's a duck."

HOW THE HIPPOPOTAMUS GOT ITS NAME

When Noah had built the ark and the time came to have all the pairs of animals go aboard, Noah named each one as it went by him up the gangplank. As a strange looking animal passed by Noah said, "The name of this animal is hippopotamus."

Noah's wife looked at him and said, "Noah, why in the world did you call that animal, that strange looking creature, a hippopotamus?"

Noah responded, "Well, it's the only one of the animals that has gone through that really looked like a hippopotamus."

REPENTANCE

A little girl had disobeyed her parents and they decided she should be punished. They took her upstairs to the bedroom, put her in the clothes closet, closed the door and said, "Now, dear, you just take time to think it over and see if you can't make up your mind to be more loving toward your parents and not disobey them."

After a few minutes, the parents' consciences began to bother them, and they went up, knocked on the door, and said, "Dear, how are you?"

"Oh, I'm fine."

"What are you doing?" asked her mother.

"Well," she replied, "I spit on your dress, I spit on your coat, I spit on your shoes, and I'm just sitting here waiting for more spit."

THE ITCHING HEAD

A boy was constantly scratching his head. His father looked at him one day and said, "Son, why are you always scratching your head?"

"Well," the boy responded, "I guess because I'm the only one who knows it itches."

HOW DO YOU FEEL TODAY?

When someone would ask, "How do you feel today, Ernest?" I well remember the reply he often gave with a little chuckle: "Well, you know, Cicero is dead, Socrates is dead, Plato is dead, and come to think of it, I don't feel so well myself."

OBSERVATIONS AT THE NUDIST COLONY

Two boys were peering over the fence observing what went on at a nudist colony. As they watched, a third boy, who was not tall enough to see over the fence, asked, "What's going on over there?"

One of the boys answered, "We don't rightly know, but they seem to be running around having a good time and lots of fun."

"What are they doing?"

"I think they're playing games."

"Are they men or women?"

"Well, we really can't tell," the boy replied. "They don't have on any clothes."

FAIR EXCHANGE

This story is about a wake which was held for a man who liked money very much. Three of his close friends sat in the front row, and after the service, as was customary, those attending passed by the open casket and placed in it a flower or some memento. Knowing of their friend's love for money, the first friend threw in a $10 bill as he filed by. The second friend did likewise. As the third friend went by he picked up both $10 bills and ceremoniously tossed in a check for $30.

THE ARTIST

A father noticed his five-year-old son studiously drawing a picture.

"Son, what are you doing?" asked the father.

"I'm drawing a picture of God."

"That's impossible," replied the father. "Nobody knows what God really looks like."

The son looked up from his drawing and said, "They'll know as soon as I finish this picture."

THE MISSING FEATHERS

A woman went to a psychologist for treatment of her delusion that she was covered with feathers. After a few sessions, the psychologist said to her, "I feel that we have gotten to the root of this problem through our discussions and analysis, and it is now behind us. What do you think, Mrs. Smith?"

"Oh," said Mrs. Smith, "I think we have had some wonderful sessions and I do feel that the problem has been taken care of. But," she added, "the only thing that bothers me now is what I'm going to do with these feathers."

She raised her hands to her shoulders and began to brush, and the psychologist suddenly jumped back. "Now, hold on just a minute, Mrs. Smith, don't you brush those feathers onto *me*."

THE BOY WHO HAD TO LEAVE HOME

There was a boy about five or six years old who had acquired the habit of using swear words in his ordinary conversation. His parents tried their best to break him of this habit and in final desperation hit upon a plan which they thought would work.

They called their son into a family consultation and laid out the facts before him, saying, "Now, son, we just can't have a little boy in our home who continues to use this kind of language. So we have decided that if you cannot break yourself of the habit, something drastic must be done. We're giving you fair warning that the very next time we hear a swear word in your conversation, you are simply going to have to pack your bag and move out of this house. We can't put up with that language any longer. Do you understand?"

He didn't say anything, although he did nod his head.

But the habit, it seemed, was too great for him to break all at once, and they soon heard him interspersing his favorite swear words in conversation.

His mother said, "Son, we gave you fair warning and now you're going to have to move out. Go pack your bag."

The boy went to his bedroom reluctantly, packed his suitcase, said goodbye to his mother, and left.

He didn't know what in the world he was going to do, so he sat on the front steps trying to collect his thoughts. As he waited there a neighbor came by, looked at him and asked, "Is your mother home, dear?"

He looked at her with a sour face and said, "How the hell should I know. I don't live here any more."

A PROPERLY PREPARED SERMON

Ernest enjoyed telling this story about a conversation which his wife, Hazel, overheard during a Sunday lecture at the Wiltern Theatre in Los Angeles, where he spoke every week to an audience of some 2300 people.

Two ladies were sitting in the row directly in front of her, and one of the ladies turned to the other, saying, "Isn't he a wonderful man and doesn't he give a wonderful talk?"

The second lady responded, "Dr. Holmes is a wonderful person and he does give a wonderful, helpful, inspirational talk each Sunday morning. But do you know, I have it on *good authority* that these wonderful talks he gives are written by his wife, Hazel Holmes!"

Both Hazel and Ernest appreciated the story, and Ernest loved to tell it with many a laugh and chuckle. What made it particularly funny to him was the fact that he never wrote a sermon, a lesson, or a lecture in his life. He did not even speak from notes, which probably was the reason he was often accused of slightly misquoting the Bible, various authors, and poets.

THE BAD HABIT THAT WASN'T

Another favorite story Ernest loved to tell on himself involved these same two ladies who sat in front of Hazel in the first balcony of the Wiltern Theatre. The first lady turned and said, "Isn't Dr. Holmes a wonderful, wonderful speaker? I so much enjoy his message each Sunday. He is so inspirational."

Her friend answered, "Yes, I quite agree. He is a wonderful man and has an inspiring message for us each Sunday. But," she said, assuming a serious tone, "it *is* a pity that he has such a drinking habit."

Surprised, the first lady said, "What a shame. I never realized that."

Her friend responded, "Yes, it is true. I have it on *good authority* that often, in the wings of the stage, they have to take Ernest and face him out in the direction of the podium. They then escort him to the stage, give him a gentle nudge, and start him on his way. And the strange part of it," she continued, "is that after he gets out there at that podium, you'd never in the world suspect he had ever had even one drink."

This was also very funny to Ernest and he enjoyed telling Hazel's version of the conversation. What made it particularly humorous to both Hazel and Ernest was that, as everyone close to him knew, he did not drink liquor in any form, and only occasionally had a glass of wine.

A PRACTICING RELIGION

The following is a true story.

Attending an interdenominational function, Ernest was sitting next to a prelate of a large Los Angeles church, who was a good friend of his. This man leaned over to Ernest and asked, "Holmes, why is it that so many of my parishioners are leaving my church to join the Religious Science Institute?"

Ernest looked at him and said, smiling, "It's really very simple. We practice what you people preach."

Venice Beach, California, 1915
Standing (l. to r.) Ernest; Fenwicke Holmes (his brother); Reginald Armor; Anne Galer (daughter of Agnes Galer).
Seated (l. to r.) Nona Brooks (Founder of Divine Science Church of Denver); Agnes Galer (Minister, Divine Science Church of Seattle; she worked with Ernest in his early lectures and ordained him as a Divine Science Minister before the Institute of Religious Science was founded); Letita Andrews (well-known metaphysical leader in Oakland, California).

Ordination service for Rev. Thomas Baird; Santa Barbara, California, 1947.
Standing (l. to r.) Ernest Tubbs (Highland Park minister); Thomas Baird; Ernest; Reginald Armor.
Seated (l. to r.) Mrs. Baird, Mrs. Holmes, Mrs. Armor.

Ernest, 1940; at home on "The Hill"—Palms, California; with his German Shepherd, Prince, and an unidentified visitor.

ERNEST HOLMES, THE MAN

Section Three
THE ELOCUTIONIST/THE POET

THE ELOCUTIONIST

Ernest Holmes was trained in the art of elocution, having graduated from the Leland Powers School of Expression in Boston. He was in his early twenties at the time, and his training involved the use of very dramatic gestures and tone of voice, as were emphasized in those early schools. His goal was to appear on the very popular Chautauqua circuit, which, under a huge tent, took outstanding speakers, dramatic readers, and actors to the people across the country.

Ernest used his flair for dramatics in lectures throughout his life, saying, "Everyone has a little ham in him, and I guess I have more than my share." And while styles changed with the passing of the years in the field of drama, Ernest retained that very expressive approach he learned early in life. His audiences sat spellbound through his presentations and thoroughly enjoyed them.

He presented his readings with feeling, often with tears of laughter or emotion rolling down his cheeks. People loved him for his humor and his sense of the dramatic, and he took great delight in his "emotional binges," particularly as they were emphasized in the reciting of his favotire poems.

An avid reader of poetry, Ernest would memorize bits of poems he liked, those which were meaningful to him, and use them extensively in his talks—although he was noted for not being particularly careful about having the exact wording of a poem. "The meaning and feeling generated are the important things," he said. Consequently, he often improvised his own words in the poems he presented during lectures. He used to say, "Don't quote me on quotes."

His early poems and readings were on subjects of a general nature—topics of the day—encompassing humor as well as pathos. Then, as time went on, he began lecturing on metaphysics, psychology, and philosophy, and his choice of poems in these lectures demonstrated his progress in thinking. Gradually, his selections reflected more and more the depth of his inner search for answers to questions about the nature of Life and God, and he became familiar with the works of outstanding poets, those who instinctively shed light on his own search for satisfactory answers in his constant quest to know *Who am I? What am I? What is my place in life?*

Although at times his choice of poems was quite thoughtful and serious, Ernest sought to maintain an evenness in his selection of material, believing there was a time to be serious and a time to introduce a light touch; a time for tears and a time for laughter. He, himself, demonstrated both of these emotions in choosing and reciting his favorite poems.

You will sense what I mean as I quote some of his favorite poems and offer comments in connection with them. As you read them, imagine this slightly chubby man reciting the lines with great emotion and considerable gesturing.

———

A fire-mist and a planet—
A crystal and a cell,
A jelly-fish and a saurian
And caves where cave-men dwell;
Then a sense of law and beauty
And a face turned from the clod,—

Some call it Evolution,
Others call it God.
　　　　　　　　—William Herbert Carruth
　　　　　　　　Each in His Own Tongue

This is one of the poems I remember Ernest reciting very early in his work—in the 1920's. He had already begun his career of lecturing and teaching classes, and we were in Boston, Massachusetts, at the time, where Robert Bitzer had a metaphysical center.

Ernest, Robert, and I were in a hotel room, and under Ernest's direction, we were all practicing elocution. First, Ernest would read William Carruth's poem, with all the feeling he could generate. Then it would be Robert's turn, followed by me. It was great fun and Robert (who later founded the Hollywood Branch of the Institute of Religious Science) and I both profited greatly from Ernest's tutelage.

———

The longer I live and the more I see
　　Of the struggle of souls toward the heights above,
The stronger this truth comes home to me:
　　That the Universe rests on the shoulders of love;
A love so limitless, deep and broad,
　　That men have renamed it and called it—God.
　　　　　　　　—Ella Wheeler Wilcox
　　　　　　　　Deathless

———

Fool! All that is, at all,
　　Lasts forever, past recall;
Earth changes, but thy soul and God stand sure:

What entered into thee
That was, is, and shall be:
Time's wheel runs back or stops: Potter and clay endure.
—Robert Browning
Rabbi Ben Ezra

———————

Our little systems have their day;
They have their day and cease to be:
They are but broken lights of Thee,
And Thou, O Lord, art more than they.
—Alfred, Lord Tennyson
In Memoriam

———————

Till a voice, as bad as Conscience, rang
interminable changes
On one everlasting Whisper day and night
repeated—so:
"Something hidden. Go and find it.
Go and look behind the Ranges—
Something lost behind the Ranges.
Lost and waiting for you. Go!"
—Rudyard Kipling
The Explorer

Ernest used only the last four lines of this poem and people
have told me they were so stimulated by his emotional reading that they felt they immediately wanted to go out and
begin their search for Reality. His very dramatic pointing
gesture at the final word—"Go"—I am sure aroused this
feeling in many persons.

———————

68

Out of the night that covers me,
*   Black as the Pit from pole to pole,*
I thank whatever Gods there be
*   For my unconquerable soul.*
                    * * *
It matters not how strait the gate,
*   How charged with punishments the scroll,*
I am the master of my fate,
*   I am the captain of my soul.*

                    —William Ernest Henley
                        Invictus

———————

. . . But what am I?
An infant crying in the night;
An infant crying for the light;
And with no language but a cry.
                    —Alfred, Lord Tennyson
                        In Memoriam, Prologue

This poem was one of Ernest's favorites and he recited it
with great feeling. To him it represented man's unfolding
awareness into the light of "Eternal Day."

———————

If I were hanged on the highest hill,
*   Mother o'mine, O mother o'mine!*
I know whose love would follow me still,
*   Mother o'mine, O mother o'mine!*

If I were drowned in the deepest sea,
*   Mother o'mine, O mother o'mine!*
I know whose tears would come down to me,
*   Mother o'mine, O mother o'mine!*

69

If I were damned of body and soul,
   Mother o'mine, O mother o'mine!
I know whose prayers would make me whole,
   Mother o'mine, O mother o'mine!
                    —Rudyard Kipling
                    Dedication

It was Ernest's custom each Mother's Day to bring his lecture to a close with this meaningful verse, which gave him an opportunity to express his deep feeling in a very dramatic manner.

Imagine this picture of what took place as Ernest demonstrated his ability to rise to great heights and then, through using the human touch, bring his listeners back to the present moment with their feet firmly planted on the ground.

Imagine him, gesturing heavenward very dramatically, arms outstretched, then returning to clasp his chest as he expressed the emotion he felt on this day of honoring motherhood. As his reading of the poem grew in intensity, tears unashamedly flowed down his cheeks.

Always following the poem there was a long silence on the part of the onlookers, as all present felt and entered into the atmosphere of love. Tears often flooded the eyes of his listeners. It was a silence charged with unutterable feeling.

After a period of silence, Ernest, as was his custom, moved from behind the lectern, placed his arm upon it as though for support, and stood looking at the audience, tears rolling down his cheeks. When it seemed as though all would burst in the tension-charged atmosphere, Ernest would reach around, take a handkerchief from his pocket and wipe the tears from his eyes. Then looking at his audience he would exclaim in a jovial voice, "Isn't it terrible to see a fat man cry!"

The spell was broken. The audience roared with laughter, with Ernest joining in.

I have always had a feeling that many persons looked forward to the Mother's Day service, when Ernest in his own dramatic manner would invariably present his Mother's Day poem.

————

When Earth's last picture is painted, and the tubes are
twisted and dried,
When the oldest colours have faded, and the youngest
critic has died,
We shall rest, and, faith, we shall need it—lie down
for an eon or two,
Till the Master of All Good Workmen shall put us to
work anew.

* * *

And only the Master shall praise us, and only the Master
shall blame;
And no one shall work for money, and no one shall work
for fame,
But each for the joy of the working, and each, in his
separate star,
Shall draw the Thing as he sees It for the God of Things
as They are.
        —Rudyard Kipling
        When Earth's Last Picture is Painted

————

71

Build thee more stately mansions, O my soul,
As the swift seasons roll!
Leave thy low-vaulted past!
Let each new temple, nobler than the last,
Shut thee from heaven with a dome more vast,
Till thou at length art free,
Leaving thine outgrown shell by life's unresting sea!
—Oliver Wendell Holmes
The Chambered Nautilus

When Ernest read this poem, as he did frequently, he pulled out all the emotional stops. His eyes were turned upward, his arms outstretched, palms open toward the "dome more vast." His voice rumbled with fervor as he rose higher and higher on his toes, and we often felt that he was about to rise above the "outgrown shell" on his way to the great unknown.

———

Let me live in my house by the side of the road
    Where the race of men go by,
They are good, they are bad, they are weak, they are strong,
    Wise, foolish—so am I.
Then why should I sit in the scorner's seat,
    Or hurl the cynic's ban?
Let me live in my house by the side of the road
    And be a friend to man.
—Sam Walter Foss
The House by the Side of the Road

———

72

I am tired of planning and toiling in the crowded lives
         of men;
Heart weary of building and spoiling, and spoiling and
         building again.
And I long for the dear old river, where I dreamed my
         youth away;
For a dreamer lives forever and a toiler dies in a day.
                           * * *
Let me dream as of old by the river, and be loved for the
         dream alway;
For a dreamer lives forever, and a toiler dies in a day.
                              —John Boyle O'Reilly
                                 The Cry of a Dreamer

———————

Bubbles we buy with a whole soul's tasking,
'Tis heaven alone that is given away,
'Tis only God may be had for the asking.
                        —James Russell Lowell
                           The Vision of Sir Launfal

———————

I used to think I knew I knew,
But now I must confess
The more I know I know,
I know I know the less.
                           —Author Unknown

THE POET

Ernest not only enjoyed reading and reciting the poetry of others, but he was also talented in his own right as a poet; because he was not especially concerned with meter or rhyme, his poems probably should be classed as blank verse. As in all his endeavors, he was persistent and turned out some excellent material.

His poetry, as with much of his writing, was done late in the evening in a special room, off by itself, which was a combination bedroom and study. It was here that he had those favorite books he used for reference and study. They were filled with notes and underscored passages. (He was never one to accumulate books just for the sake of having a large library. While he did purchase and read all the latest books on religion, philosophy, science, psychology, etc., as they were published, he kept only those he felt he would use for reference. He gave the others away.)

He did his late-night writing propped up in bed, with several pillows cushioning him, after the household had become quiet. He would use a wooden clipboard for a writing surface, and for paper, whatever was handy. He saved the cardboard inserts that accompanied his laundered shirts and used them regularly for his compositions.

I remember that he wore a visor, usually green, which fitted around his head, shading his eyes from the glare of the light which was clamped to the headboard of the bed.

This is not the picture of the classic poet, sitting under a tree with a chirping chorus of nature's sounds to inspire him, but this was Ernest's way.

He became proficient in writing inspirational poems, many of which were published by one of the country's finest greeting-card publishers. They expressed his sentimental thoughts on friendship, love, and special occasions such as birthdays, Mother's Day, anniversaries, etc. A number of them were set to music by friends who were outstanding composers.

What is considered some of his finest poetry appeared in the classic epic poem written in collaboration with his brother, Fenwicke. This volume, *The Voice Celestial* (now out of print), illustrates the basic teaching evolved by Ernest Holmes and embraces many of the classic philosophies and religious teachings of the ages. Ernest spent many years on this creative effort and considered it one of his best literary accomplishments.

The Voice Celestial is the story of everyman's journey on the pathway of life—his questions, his doubts, perplexities, insights into the happenings which take place in his search, and finally his emergence into a spiritual knowledge of the truth of his being. The inner awareness of the complete unity of man and God, called Cosmic Consciousness—an experience felt by all the great mystics of the ages—is graphically described.

The Voice Celestial vividly represents the journey of the soul and I would be remiss if I did not include some excerpts from it. These excerpts represent a dialogue between man, the traveler on the journey of life, and the inner voice, or the "Presence" that is Spirit within each man. As we read these particular quotes, let us think, as Ernest would have urged, of the Presence within each of us, awaiting our acceptance of Its guidance and inspiration.

Ernest also wrote the lyrics for many songs, some of which were published in the *Religious Science Hymnal.* I

quote several of these, along with some of his rather sentimental and inspiring poems.

Excerpts from *The Voice Celestial*

God gave Himself when He gave life to all
And givingness itself must answer to the call
Of need, and givingness to be complete
Includes forgivingness . . . .
This all the great and good and wise have known,
He who forgives shall have forgivingness shown.
Clear thou thy heart from grudge against another,
Act toward thy foe as if he were thy brother . . . .
Look long and earnestly upon each man
Until you pierce the outer shell and can
Behold in him the hidden soul and see
How like he is to God; seek for Me!

(Page 183)

Love has a thousand names, a thousand ways
But in all forms resolves itself to this:
Love is the union of two kindred things
Each with each and all with each, and all with all.
When you shall see yourself in every one
You meet and *feel this union,* and care
For him because he has a need which you
Can fill, you have become a lover of
The Me, a self devoted to the higher self.

(Page 181)

Too oft in fear man looks at God as Force
With Whom there is no mode of intercourse,
Yet all the time this perfect Love stands by
With outstretched hand behind the darkest sky . . . .
The gift of love is freedom under law:
God knows no pain because He breaks no law,
In harmony with love. But giving man
The power of choice, He sets him free
To keep or break the law of harmony.

(Page 187)

Once more I say to you, you need not wait
For heaven, for heaven waits for you, and it
Is now. Immortal life is *here* and he
Who has through love found life within the Me
Resolves all doubts and solves life's mystery.

(Page 190)

Whosoever comes with lowly heart to God,
Be he of Krishna, Buddha, Moses, Christ,
He will not fail to see! How sweet the words
The lamp of love for man is lit,
And *man* walks in the light of it;
From here to the Eternal Shore,
The circled beam will go before.

(Page 160)

Men pray for *good* but when it comes, the door
Is shut by self-abasement or by doubt.
They had the faith to ask; but not enough
To quite accept the gift—Here one accepts
And his deep wounds are healed; God hears each call
But cannot force your hand to take the gift
For which you prayed. Another asks for full

Supply for daily needs and streams of plenty
Swirl around his door. And some do pray
With hope but no expectancy and they
Do not receive, "Ye must believe ye have
Received (I promise you) ye shall receive."

(Page 150)

Be not afraid to look for truth within;
No avatars nor "shade," nor "guide," nor Soul
Returned from astral planes to haunt your room
And give you sage advice has wisdom to
Impart what equals that which you can find
Within, when once you listen to the Me.

Enlarge, expand awareness of thy cosmic self;
Not God made small but man made great doth solve
The riddle of the Universe, for
THOU ART THAT.

(Page 169)

These poems by Ernest are lyrics of hymns appearing in
The Religious Science Hymnal. *

SONG OF PRAISE

Let our song of praise arise
Filling earth and air and skies.
Let all earth awake and sing
While the heavenly echoes ring.

Dodd, Mead & Co., New York. © 1954, International Association of Religious Science Churches. Used by permission.

Though we tarry here below
As the seasons come and go,
Still our lives are one in Thee,
Bless this perfect Unity.

Morning dawns so fair and calm,
Free from sorrow, free from harm.
Evening comes at love's behest
When day's labor sinks to rest.
Bless the morning, noon and night
Filled with beauty, warmth and light.
Bless this life that came from Thee,
Father through Eternity.

LIFE OF MY LIFE

Life of my life, O Love Divine,
I am the branch, Thou art the vine.
No far or near, no depth or height,
Can keep me from Thy perfect sight.
At break of dawn, at noon and night,
The thought of Thee burns warm and bright.
In midnight hush, Thy presence near
Keeps me from harm, and doubt and fear.

In Thee I live, O blessed thought.
There is no place where Thou art not.
Through all that lives, one Presence runs
Through endless times and earths and suns.
O wonderous thought that Life Divine
Should with our life Itself entwine.
No act of man that need atone.
For Thou art all and all alone.

IN ONE ACCORD

In one accord, our voices raise
A song of joy, a hymn of praise,
To the Everlasting One,
To God the Father, God the Son.

Breath of breath, and heart of heart,
Of all that lives, eternal part,
Bless this life that love has given
And bless this union, born of heaven.

Here on earth our joy to be,
Forever joined in truth with Thee,
One in body, mind and soul
With the Spirit of the whole.

While we chant our evening prayer
To a Father's love and care,
Lords of Light their vigil keep
As in the arms of love we sleep.

BE STILL AND KNOW

"Be still and know that I am God,
Be still and know that I am God."
I am quiet and peaceful for I put my trust in Thee,
A great stillness steals over me,
And a great calm quiets my whole being
As I realize Thy Presence, Thy Presence in me.
I am still in Thy Presence,
And I put my whole confidence in Thee alone.

The following poems were set to music by Richard Froeber.

THE SONG OF THE HEART

Let the song on your lips be a happy thing
For the song of the heart is the song to sing.
So never let go but smile your smile
And you'll live on earth for a long, long while.
It's the man with a smile with his lips upcurled
Who will win all the love of the whole wide world.
The song of the heart is the only thing
That will keep you young, so sing, boy, sing.

IF YOU HAVE A GIFT, BRING IT

If you have a gift, bring it,
If you have a song, sing it,
If you have a talent, use it,
If you have love, diffuse it.

If you have a prayer, pray it,
If you have a kind word, say it,
If you have a religion, live it,
If you have happiness, give it.

I SAID A PRAYER

I said a prayer for you today,
    A simple prayer I often pray.
A prayer I always like to say
    For those I meet along the way.

This prayer, my friend, was just for you,
    That you'll be blessed in all you do,
In everything that you pursue;
    And may all your dreams come true.
I said a prayer for you today.

81

Ernest; William H. D. Hornaday; Reginald Armor (1957).

Ernest Holmes, the man: circa 1950.

ERNEST HOLMES, THE MAN

Section Four
THE AUTHOR

Some of His Heretofore Unpublished
Observations on Philosophy,
Religion, and Metaphysics

The Author:
Philosopher, Religionist, and Metaphysician

Ernest Holmes wrote voluminously on those subjects to which he devoted his life. His writing followed the pattern of his lectures and teachings, being devoted principally to philosophy, religion, psychology, and the metaphysical/scientific approach to life.

He never believed he was an outstanding author, and although he acknowledged that pure inspiration played a significant role in his literary efforts, he always emphasized that hard work and persistence were also a part of his creative efforts.

While he did not often isolate himself from life, when there was writing to be done he did spend much time alone in his bedroom-study or in his office, where his thoughts would not be interrupted. Because people sometimes used the hall door to his office at the Institute to bypass his secrtary, he frequently tacked a sheet of paper to the door on which he wrote, "Busy, do not disturb."

His first writing experience involved composing on a portable typewriter, but because he was not a skilled typist, he found that using a machine, plus the inevitable mistakes, interrupted his train of thought. "It does not keep up with my ideas," he complained.

He later dictated to a secretary, a process which seemed to work out better.

Ernest never used any particular technique for structuring his work, and he usually did not use outlines, as the writing experts would have advised. Ordinarily, he would gather up his rough-draft notes, read them aloud ("That gives me a sense of how they will be received by others"), and then make whatever changes were necessary to put them in final shape. Often, he worked the material over many, many times before he felt satisfied with the result.

When he was finished with something new and was satisfied with it, he would usually concede modestly that it was pretty good, then turn it over to someone who checked it for accuracy of grammar—and he immediately forgot about it and went on to something else. He was not one to continue searching for any flaws. "Let it stand on the merit it has," he would say.

Another of his favorite methods of composing books was to have his lectures, church services, and teaching sessions taken down in shorthand (later by tape recording) and transcribed. But this was time-consuming, requiring a lot of rewriting and effort. "The darn things never come out on paper the way they sound when I am giving them," he protested. As a result of this process, however, he gleaned from his spoken material many worthwhile statements which he would later assemble in book form. He worked hours on end with these transcribed lectures, propped up in bed in his bedroom-study, wearing his green eye shade to keep the bright light softened.

The following section consists of excerpts from these transcribed lectures. I was fortunate to be named under the terms of Ernest's will to inherit certain rights to the material, which had been edited by him to be put in book form at a later time. Science of Mind Publications has since assembled and published much of it, although I recently became aware of a file of some transcribed notes which had been misplaced.

I feel that among these items are many gems of philosophical thinking which should be shared with others. They are dynamic statements, expressing Ernest's personal ideas and inspirations on subjects that were close to his heart, giving us an added insight into Ernest Holmes, the man.

PHILOSOPHY

The intuitive motivations and spiritual realizations of the ages are more powerful than all intellectual denials of them.

God made all days—all days are His days; therefore, all days are good days.

We look upon the objective form of God in the mountain, the sunset, the glory of the storm, the strength of the wind and wave; and the thing in us that does the looking is an indwelling Presence.

Our possessions too often possess us. We shall only keep what we give. The law of Nature is *use* or *lose.*

A philosophy of materialism never yet created a great work of art, a great religion, or a great anything.

What we call the physical world is Spirit in form, forever flowing.

When all the nations of the world see God incarnated in each other, they will no longer have use for swords.

When the collective intelligence of the human race arrives at a concept of freedom, the human race will be free, and not until then. There may be those who believe we can compel freedom, but we cannot do so. We would only find ourselves exchanging one kind of bondage for another.

Every man at times feels that if he could open some door which appears to be closed, he would step instantly into a larger life. This is the borderland of Cosmic Consciousness. Some people travel close to It the greater part of the time, and even the ones who stand back in the shadows, denying Its existence, hope It is so.

If we look at love long enough, we shall become lovely.

The spiritual world contains an image of the physical; the physical is a counterpart of the spiritual.

Love is an essence, an atmosphere, which defies analysis, as does Life Itself.

Love fires the heart, stimulates the emotions, renews the soul, and proclaims the Spirit.

Love is the central Flame of the universe, nay, the very Fire Itself.

The Father's house is always open, the latchstring ever hanging out, the door always ajar, but man himself must enter if he wishes to abide within.

Those who have given the best to the world have always been best remembered by it, and most loved throughout the ages.

Self-effacement, the neglect of the body, or the belief that we must be unhappy in order to serve Truth, are immature ideas which deny the Divine birthright of the soul, the incarnated Spirit of the Most High within us.

It is impossible for a man to conceal himself. In every act, word, or gesture he stands revealed as he is, and not as he would have himself appear to be.

Let the one who is sad or depressed find some purpose into which he may pour his whole being and he will find a new inflow of life, one of which he has never dreamed.

To suppose an eternity without the element of time is to suppose an impossibility, for it means to suppose an unexpressed existence.

We are in the midst of Supreme Intelligence. It presses against the doors of our thought, waiting to be known.

Each step in advance is an eternal step and will never have to be taken again. We are not building for a day or a year, but for all time, for Eternity.

Great men are those who have a vision and then go to work to make it come true, never looking away from it, but with one-pointedness and calm determination sticking to an idea until it becomes an accomplished fact.

The wide-awake person can find so many things to do that he hasn't time even to begin doing them in this life. Eternity is necessary to carry out the ideals that he already has evolved.

Evil is a personal problem, not a Cosmic one.

No man can demonstrate peace while he is unhappy. He can demonstrate a resignation which he calls peace, but it won't be peace.

Each of us is more or less an individualized personification of the entire history of the human race.

All change takes place within the Changeless; all form appears within the Formless; all movement is in That which is without movement.

If we wish to discover the nature of the abstract, we must analyze the nature of the concrete. If we wish to understand the nature of the Universal Mind, we must analyze the nature of the individual mind.

Spirit is both the center and circumference of everything.

Evolution does not create intelligence. Intelligence creates evolution.

To the pure the universe is pure. To the impure, the universe is impure.

The possibilities in the play of Life upon Itself are so great that a man may elevate his consciousness to heaven or descend into hell by standing on different rungs of the same ladder.

The Originating Power descends into the consciousness which meditates upon It and receives It. The intellect then abandons itself to the Divine. This is a feeling, a sense, an atmosphere.

The Almighty has implanted genius within the soul of everyone.

God has no pets—the kingdom of heaven is not a household of God's personal favorites.

Let us never think that waving a banner, singing a psalm, or putting on a pageant can take the place of interior conviction, a silent looking into our own soul.

The devil is a fiction, a myth, a vacuum, a nothing.

It isn't the soul that grows old, or the mind; it is the thought that grows old.

God speaks only to the ear that listens.

We are members of everyman's religion. Buddhist, Confucian, Mohammedan, Jew, and Christian, and even the pagan—all partake of the same Divine Life; each has *his* road to good, to the Divinity that is latent within everyone.

RELIGION

Prayer to God is communion with an Inner Life, with the divine indwelling Spirit, which is everywhere present, omnipotent, and all-powerful.

Everything we see is God—the buttercup, the sunset, the morning dew nestling in the petal of a rose; and love and laughter, they are God. God is the innermost Presence, the outermost Rim and Circumference of our experience.

I do not believe any man can really be happy unless he believes in the continuity of his own existence. It is impossible for a man to be contented in this life unless he feels sure of the next one.

There is no special dispensation of Providence, there is no God who cares more for one than for another. As intelligent beings we must realize that God is a universal Presence, a neutral Force, an impersonal Observer, a divine and impartial Giver, forever pouring Himself or Itself upon His or Its creation.

The illumined have never lost their identity. Cosmic Consciousness has not come through psychic confusion and no man has ever been spiritually illumined in the psychic realm alone.

The gift of heaven is Life, not death; Love, not hate; Peace, not confusion.

Love overcomes everything and neutralizes all that is unlike Itself.

To pray without ceasing is to doubt never, but to always trust in the Law of Good.

By man alone come mistakes. By man alone comes salvation.

Christ and Adam are two different names for the same man; one is earthly, the other is heavenly. Adam typifies the material man, while Christ typifies the spiritual man. Each of us is both Adam and Christ. We die daily in Adam and daily we are resurrected in Christ.

All the tomorrows that stretch down the vistas of eternity will be but a continuity of our own experiences. We shall keep on keeping on. We shall continue in our own individual stream of consciousness, while forever and ever expanding.

There is no sin but a mistake and no punishment but a consequence.

There was never an illumined soul who has not taught the final and complete emancipation of all from evil. Any religion that casts a shadow across the final deliverance of everyman's soul was born out of chaos.

When we use the word "God," we mean that Universal Intelligence, that Universal Life Principle, that Spirit or Creative Cause which runs through everything, which unites everything, which is the Power and the Presence in everything, and which yet forever remains more than anything in which It incarnates.

If we have sinned, it is because we have been ignorant of our true nature, a recognition of which is necessary to bring us to ourselves.

Because of the unity underlying all life, no man lives entirely unto himself, but through himself he individualizes the Whole, which Whole includes all other lives.

Eventually, Love overcometh and exalteth Itself above all, for Love is a synonym for the Eternal Heart of the Universe.

Spirituality is simple goodness, human kindness, natural truth, brotherly love, and heavenly worship. To be spiritual is to be normal.

Men will come and men will go, friend and foe alike may fall away, but always the soul shall be thrown back upon itself. The Indwelling Spirit that lives in the secret place of our lives will ever be with us.

We need not be afraid of religion. What we wish to avoid is not religion, but dogmatism and superstition. We avoid these by keeping faith with reason, for it converts the soul to Reality, gives peace to the mind, and joy to the heart.

Man is a center of God in God. Whatever God is in the Universal, man must be in the individual world. The difference between God and man is one of degree and not of essence.

I AM is a name given to the Infinite. I AM and I am you; I AM and I am the rose; I AM and I am the caterpillar; I AM and I am the picture on the wall; I AM all there is, beside which there is none other.

One of the wisest things a person can do is to forgive himself all his mistakes and to do this until he finds release.

The Real Man is perfect, the Real Man is spiritual, the Real Man is the essence of God—manifesting as individuality.

Spirituality is not something we acquire; it is something we express.

Above all, learn tolerance.

METAPHYSICS

No treatment is as good as it ought to be if the one giving it feels that the demonstration is dependent on anything in the objective world. It is only as we know that we are truly using a *spiritual* Law that our treatment is effective.

We need to learn that evil is not person, place, or thing, but is an experience which we are allowed to have because of our Divine individuality. We suffer from negative experience until we learn to use the Law affirmatively, to cooperate with It, and thus to enjoy Its full benefits. The true Law is a law of liberty and not a law of bondage.

Universal Spirit is perfect in us, through us, and around us, although our finite psychological nature modifies Its perfect flow through us. Therefore, It appears to us in the form of the images of our own thought, but those images are formed by our previous experience and what the world has believed. They are not necessarily Truth.

There is only One Mind. We use that Mind and where we use It we call that place *our* mind.

If we are but the sum total of our psychological reactions, what was it that antedated the first psychological reaction? Man existed before he psychologized himself. Spirit is antecedent to any reaction to It. The spirit in man existed before he consciously became aware of It.

A silent conviction of Truth is worth more than the loudest proclamations of those who shout affirmations to the great nowhere.

There is One Thinker, thinking through all of us. This Universal Thinker is incarnated in everyone. Every person has access to It; every person uses It, whether ignorantly or consciously.

The body is a reflection of the soul. When the soul is illumined by the Spirit, the Spirit quickens the mortal part of us and heals the body.

Whatever the mind firmly believes forms a pattern of thought, a creative mold. Whatever is in the mind tends to take outward form. This is the secret of the creative Law of Mind.

Man's mind should swing from inspiration to action, from contemplation to accomplishment, from prayer to performance.

The Spirit fires the soul with energy and understanding; the soul vitalizes the body and animates all that we do.

Today is good. Tomorrow will be good. And that vista of tomorrows which stretches down the bright eternity of an endless future will be good.

As much gathers more, as like attracts like, so success breeds success.

See the Reality hidden behind the veil of illusion.

If we can bring our mind to a place where it no longer conceives evil, then evil cannot exist for us.

How often we condemn when we should forgive, how often we censure when we might praise. What untold grief of heart might be relieved by words of cheer and forgiveness.

103

Let us judge no one, condemn no one, but realize that all are on the road of experience, seeking the same goal, and that each must ultimately find his home in the Spirit.

Man, as the image of eternity, is made of God-stuff. He partakes of the Divine Nature. On the scale of the individual he reproduces the Universal. As God is in the big world, so man is in the little world; a small circle within an Infinite One; the same elements, the same Nature.

Man can learn only through experience, until the time comes that he is in complete unity with God. Then he will know without first having experienced.

Our thought is the seed and Mind is the soil.

It will relieve the overworked brain and the tired muscle just to be still and know that we are One with the All-in-All.

Sooner or later the Law of the Absolute Justice weighs out to each person his own measure.

As water reaches its own level, so our outward conditions reproduce our inner realizations.

We free ourselves through the same Law by which we first bound ourselves.

A calm determination to think exactly what we want to think, regardless of conditions, will do much to put us on the highway toward a greater realization of Life.

Believing is necessary because all is Mind, and until we have provided a full acceptance, we have not made a mold into which Mind can pour Itself, through which It can manifest.

For selfish reasons alone, we cannot afford to hate or even to hold anything against any living soul.

I desire to understand all people and that desire is reflected back to me from all people. I help, therefore I am helped. I uplift, therefore I am uplifted.

God's world is not a world of illusion but one of Divine realities. Our knowledge of Truth does not explain *away* things that we see; it explains what they are.

Though the whole world has suffered a sense of limitation, there is no limitation to the Universe. When all people know the Truth—ways, methods, and means will be found for the freedom of all people.

When evolution brings the thing evolving to the place where it can reflect on its own states of consciousness, the incarnation of Spirit produces personality and that thing becomes man—a self-choosing center.

There is no medium between us and the Universal Mind but our own thought.

As we leave confusions behind and enter into the Presence, we become peaceful. Of Itself, Law is neither peace nor confusion. It is a mirror. If we hold an object in front of a mirror, the image in the mirror is that of the object.

The Universal Spirit is the Supreme Knower, while the Law can only operate on that which is known.

106

We must transcend the appearance, even though we admit it as a fact.

The Infinite is beyond our comprehension and yet that which we do comprehend *is* the Infinite at the level of such comprehension.

An absent treatment is no different from a present one because there can be no absence in Universal Presence. It is always at the point of our perception, and all of It is there.

What Mind knows in one place, It knows simultaneously in all places, and instantly.

One of the chief characteristics of subjectivity is that it is conscious but it is not self-conscious. It is intelligent but it does not know it does what it does.

When we deal with subjectivity we are always dealing with that which is subject to control by conscious volition.

What I call my subjective mind is merely the place where Subjectivity Itself reacts to my personal use of It.

There are no such things as good and evil of themselves. But unless we have the privilege of experiencing the undesirable as well as the desirable, we can have only the possibility of experiencing by compulsion and not by choice. This is the only way we can be individuals.

The absolute freedom of our *own* nature is so complete that bondage is but a negative expression of that complete freedom.

Creation is an eternal function of the Mind of God. It is the Self-knowledge of Spirit in action.

The Infinite cannot know time as separated from eternity; mortality as separated from immortality. It can know incident, but not time. It knows experience without knowing duration.

We are centers of God-consciousness in a Universal Mind, using the Mind we are in. This Mind is one Mind. The places where you and I use It individualize It, stamping It with the uniqueness of our own individual selves, therefore personalizing It as us.

No two people are alike and yet all people are rooted in the One.

Thought is spontaneous when it is created. What happens to it from then on is entirely mechanical.

The more convinced we are that there is an ever-present Goodness, an omniscient Goodness, an all-powerful Goodness that instantly springs into action through our word, the more power our word will have.

Conscious thought can definitely change subjective trends in our own minds and in the minds of those for whom we are treating. This is what spiritual mind treatment is. It is reversing the order of thought, neutralizing wrong thought, and through the creation of a new pattern of thinking, making possible a greater outflow of that Life which is already at the center of every person. Treatment is an opening up of the consciousness rather than a reaching out for something external. It is loosing it rather than capturing it.

It seems to me that God lets us alone until we discover God, and when we discover God, we discover ourselves at the same time.

Subtly, the opinions of those around us stay in us, remain with us, and seek to manifest through the logical functioning of the creative agencies of our own mind.

Have no fear of tomorrow; enjoy today. Refuse to carry the corpse of a mistaken yesterday. What misery is suffered through the burdens imposed by yesterday and the bitter fears of tomorrow!

AFTERWORD

In this book I have sought to illustrate many facets of Ernest Holmes' thinking, his opinions, speculations, and insights into Truth. I have endeavored to portray him as he would want to be known and understood—not a mysterious or inaccessible person, but a normal individual searching for Truth in all of life and living.

Ernest Holmes, the man, has passed from the scene, but the words, the teachings, and the wisdom of this very warm, natural person will live long in the minds and hearts of humanity. Because he was always himself, his lengthened shadow will increasingly reach out to many of us who tread the path of unfoldment of the One Life and the One Presence, which Ernest saw so clearly is within each of us.